DATE DUE

Children of the World
Nicaragua

For their help in the preparation of *Children of the World: Nicaragua*, the editors gratefully thank the Sandinista Children's Association and Escuela Teresa Arce, León, Nicaragua; Project Minnesota-León; the Embassy of Nicaragua (Canada), Ottawa, Ontario; Professor Howard Handelman, University of Wisconsin-Milwaukee; and Professor Michael Fleet, Marquette University, Milwaukee.

Flag illustration on page 48, © Flag Research Center.

Library of Congress Cataloging-in-Publication Data

Cummins, Ronald.
     Nicaragua / photography by Rose Welch; written by Ronnie Cummins.
        p. cm. — (Children of the world)
     Includes bibliographical references.
     Summary: Presents the life of a ten-year-old boy and his family in Nicaragua, describing his home and school activities and discussing the history, geography, ethnic composition, natural resources, languages, government, religions, culture, and economics of his country.
     ISBN 0-8368-0221-7
     1. Nicaragua—Social life and customs—Juvenile literature. 2. Children—Nicaragua—Juvenile literature. [1. Family life—Nicaragua. 2. Nicaragua.] I. Welch, Rose, ill. II. Title. III. Series: Children of the world (Milwaukee, Wis.)
     F1523.8.C86   1990
     972.85—dc20   89-43174

A Gareth Stevens Children's Books edition
Edited, designed, and produced by

Gareth Stevens Children's Books
RiverCenter Building, Suite 201
1555 North RiverCenter Drive
Milwaukee, Wisconsin 53212, USA

Series editor: Valerie Weber
Editor: Amy Bauman
Research editor: Kathleen Weisfeld Barrilleaux
Designer: Laurie Shock
Map design: Sheri Gibbs

Printed in the United States of America

1 2 3 4 5 6 7 8 9 96 95 94 93 92 91 90

Children of the World
Nicaragua

Text by Ronnie Cummins
Photography by Rose Welch

Gareth Stevens Children's Books
MILWAUKEE

. . . a note about *Children of the World*:

The children of the world live in fishing towns, Arctic regions, and urban centers, on islands and in mountain valleys, on sheep ranches and fruit farms. This series follows one child in each country through the pattern of his or her life. Candid photographs show the children with their families, at school, at play, and in their communities. The text describes the dreams of the children and, often through their own words, tells how they see themselves and their lives.

Each book also explores events that are unique to the country in which the child lives, including festivals, religious ceremonies, and national holidays. The *Children of the World* series does more than tell about foreign countries. It introduces the children of each country and shows readers what it is like to be a child in that country.

Children of the World includes the following published and soon-to-be-published titles:

Australia	El Salvador	Japan	Spain
Bhutan	England	Jordan	Sweden
Bolivia	Finland	Malaysia	Tanzania
Brazil	France	Mexico	Thailand
Burkina Faso	Greece	Nepal	Turkey
Burma	Guatemala	New Zealand	USSR
China	Hong Kong	Nicaragua	Vietnam
Costa Rica	Hungary	Philippines	West Germany
Cuba	India	Singapore	Yugoslavia
Czechoslovakia	Indonesia	South Africa	Zambia
Egypt	Italy	South Korea	

. . . and about *Nicaragua*:

Ten-year-old Michael Eduardo Chávez Garcia lives with his mother, grandparents, aunts, uncles, and cousins in San Jerónimo, a neighborhood on the outskirts of León, Nicaragua's second largest city. Although the homes in San Jerónimo are poor by North American standards, the people who live there feel that conditions are improving, and Michael enjoys being surrounded by so many friends and family members.

To enhance this book's value in libraries and classrooms, comprehensive reference sections include up-to-date data about Nicaragua's geography, demographics, currency, education, culture, industry, and natural resources. *Nicaragua* also features a bibliography, research topics, activity projects, and discussions of such subjects as Managua, the country's history, political system, ethnic and religious composition, and language.

The living conditions and experiences of children in Nicaragua vary according to economic, environmental, and ethnic circumstances. The reference sections help bring to life for young readers the diversity and richness of the culture and heritage of Nicaragua. Of particular interest are discussions of the changes in Nicaragua since its revolution and its relationship with other nations throughout the Americas.

CONTENTS

Michael (lower right) and his mother, Daisy (far right), pose with some of their relatives.

North America

Nicaragua

South America

Europe

Asia

Africa

Australia

Republic of Nicaragua

Mexico

Caribbean Sea

Belize

Honduras

León

Guatemala

El Salvador

Costa Rica

Pacific Ocean

Panama

LIVING IN NICARAGUA:
Michael, a Boy from León

Ten-year-old Michael Eduardo Chávez Garcia lives in the city of León, Nicaragua. With a population of over 130,000, León is the second largest city in the country. Michael lives with his mother, grandparents, aunts, uncles, and cousins in San Jerónimo, a neighborhood on the outskirts of León.

A total of 34 of Michael's relatives live in four houses in the neighborhood. Chávez Street — the street on which Michael lives — is named in honor of his father, who was killed while fighting in the Nicaraguan revolution of 1979. This all happened just before Michael was born.

For Michael and most of his relatives, it is only a ten-minute bus ride into León to go to work or to school. Michael's grandfather, Jésus Chávez, works 25 miles (40 km) away, where he tends the family's cornfield and vegetable garden.

From a rooftop, Michael looks out over the sprawling city of León.

Set amid Nicaragua's rolling hills and dense greenery, León is a city rich in history.

A horse-drawn vendor's cart rolls past Michael's house in San Jerónimo.

At Home in San Jerónimo

Michael's family has lived in the *barrio*, or neighborhood, of San Jerónimo for the past 22 years. Michael likes living in San Jerónimo because he is surrounded by many cousins and friends his own age. He can always find enough people to play a game of baseball or soccer. When not playing or doing his chores, Michael and his cousins attend school in León, where all of his aunts and uncles work.

All of the families in San Jerónimo are poor by North American standards. The streets are unpaved and dusty, and almost no one has a car. Most of the houses need painting. Though it's very hot here most of the year, no one has an air conditioner, and fans are rare. Still, the Chávez family and their neighbors say that conditions in Nicaragua are improving. Many families — including Michael's — now have indoor plumbing and running water in their homes.

One advantage of living in an extended family is that Michael can always find someone to play with. Here, Michael and his cousins play in the courtyard of the Chávez home. The children often spend the hot afternoons in the courtyard, which is usually the coolest spot in the house.

Many families in San Jerónimo own their house. Michael's family, however, rents a house that is shared by nine relatives. Many people live in extended families such as Michael's. By living together and working hard, families are surviving Nicaragua's hard times. The Chávez house is a typical five-room dwelling, in which everyone must share one bedroom. Made of cement blocks, it has a tin roof and surrounds a small courtyard. It also has a partially enclosed kitchen and lots of ventilation because it gets so hot in León.

Michael's house is simple. Although the house has electricity, the family does not own a television. So some evenings, Michael goes to a friend's house to watch television. But more often, he listens to the radio, hoping to catch baseball scores. The Chávez house doesn't have a phone either, but no one in the neighborhood has a private telephone. Everyone relies on the public telephone on the outer wall of the Chávez house.

Michael proudly shows visitors the memorial to his father that stands in front of his home.

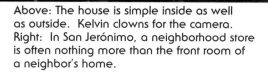

Above: The house is simple inside as well
as outside. Kelvin clowns for the camera.
Right: In San Jerónimo, a neighborhood store
is often nothing more than the front room of
a neighbor's home.

San Jerónimo has no large stores
or supermarkets. One of the
neighboring families runs a
store, called a *tienda*, from
inside their house. On hot days,
Michael buys a sweetened corn
drink, called a *chi-cha*. Here
he may also buy his favorite
candy, called *cajeta*. Most
candy in Nicaragua is homemade.
Michael would find it funny that
candy in other countries is often
made in a factory.

Off to Work and School

Everyone gets up early in the Chávez house. The morning, with its cool, pleasant air, is Michael's favorite time of day, and he usually gets up by 5:30 a.m. While his grandmother Emelina makes tortillas and prepares breakfast, Michael finishes up his homework and gets ready for school. If he has time, he even does a few chores around the house. One of his chores is to feed his pet parrot, Laura. As he feeds her, Michael talks to her, and sometimes she seems to chatter back to him.

After a breakfast of rice, beans, and fried bananas, Michael and his mother walk to the bus stop together. The bus ride into León costs 500 *córdobas* (equivalent to about five cents). Once in León, Michael's mother walks him to his school. Then she walks a few more blocks to her job at the Children's Association headquarters.

Preparing meals is no simple task. To make the corn tortillas, Emelina must first grind kernels of corn in a hand grinder. With the ground corn, she then makes a dough that is shaped into the typical round, flat cake and cooked over an open fire.

While Emelina prepares breakfast, Michael is busy with morning chores, such as making his bed, washing dishes, and feeding his parrot, Laura. For fun, Michael tries to finish his chores before his grandmother calls him to the table, but he doesn't often beat her.

Michael and his fourth-grade class stand still long enough to pose for a class photo in front of the Escuela Teresa Arce.

Michael's School: The Escuela Teresa Arce

Michael is in the fourth grade at Escuela Teresa Arce. *Escuela* is Spanish for "school." Michael's school is named after Teresa Arce, a popular teacher who taught at the school for many years. Since almost everyone in Michael's family has attended Escuela Teresa Arce, the school has played a central role in the family's lives. Because of this, Michael's mother, Daisy, and other parents sometimes do volunteer work at the school. Right now, on weekends, a group of parents is fixing the school's roof before the rainy season begins.

Although he's a bit shy, Michael likes going to school and being with his classmates. History and math are his favorite subjects. According to his teacher, Indiana Castillo Martinez, Michael studies hard and gets some of the best grades in the class. Michael spends several hours every day reading and doing homework.

Left: Michael puts a lot of time into his studies. Because math is one of his favorite subjects, he always tries to work the problems through by himself before asking for help. Below: The table is often one mass of books, papers, and supplies.

Michael and his classmates take turns reading aloud from one of their textbooks.
Although Michael reads well, he is very nervous when his turn comes.

One of the subjects that is stressed in school is Nicaraguan and Central American history. The city of León has a long, interesting history. It was founded by Spanish colonists in 1524, which makes it one of the oldest cities in the Americas. The city has many museums and historical sites, most of them within walking distance of Michael's school.

Like many Nicaraguan students, Michael wears a uniform to school. The uniforms, like the books and other supplies, are given to the students free of charge. This makes it easier for even the poorest parents to send their children to school. Because there is a shortage of school buildings and classrooms, Nicaraguan schools usually run in two shifts. Michael attends the morning shift from 7:30 a.m. until 12:30 p.m. The older students go from 12:30 p.m. until 5:30 p.m. Michael is glad to be on the morning shift; finishing school just after noon leaves most of the day ahead of him.

For these girls a uniform consists of a white blouse and a dark skirt. ▶

At 9:30 a.m., the fourth-graders have recess. This gives Michael time to talk with his friends or just run around the courtyard. After being cooped up in the classroom, it's fun to act kind of wild. But after an exciting game of tag, it feels just as good to cool off in the shade. Sometimes, Michael likes a quieter game; then he plays marbles.

Three days a week, a physical education teacher comes into the school after recess. Then all the students exercise together and play different sports. Of all sports, Michael likes baseball the best.

◀ Someone is always coming up with a new game to play at recess.

Below: Recess or physical education? Sometimes it's hard to tell the difference.

Watering the plants on the patio is one of
Michael's afternoon chores. He tries not to rush
through them, even though he knows that his
cousins are waiting for him.

Back at the office, Daisy wonders what Michael
is doing at home.

School's Out!

Michael's mother, Daisy, is a bookkeeper for the Children's
Association. Her job is to keep track of the association's income
and expenses, and she finds it interesting work. When school
ends at 12:30, Michael walks to his mother's office. Together,
they ride the bus back to San Jerónimo.

After lunch, Daisy must return to the office, but Michael stays home.
He has homework and chores to do, but when he is finished, he
will still have plenty of time for play. Michael and his cousins
Kelvin, Guerman, and Yuardin always find something to do. Of
all the games they play, Michael's favorites are baseball, marbles,
and checkers. Sometimes, Kelvin brings his bicycle, which has a
passenger seat in back. Michael and Kelvin take turns pedaling
as they zip around the neighborhood.

Right: Kelvin takes Michael for a spin on his bicycle, hoping that the ride will cool them. Below: Michael thinks that a game of checkers is always a good way to spend the afternoon — especially when he wins.

23

Michael Takes a Walking Tour of León

As part of a special history project in school, Michael is taking tours of León's historical sites on weekends. Accompanied by his mother and younger cousins, Michael begins today's tour in the city's central park. From here, horse-drawn cabs run regularly to all parts of the city. Michael prefers taking these to riding the city buses. Although the buses are faster, the horses are a lot more fun.

Today's first stop is the Indian neighborhood of Subtiava, where he sees the ruins of the church of Vera Cruz. Michael and his cousins explore the crumbling church, climbing in and out of its ruins. Nearby is Santa Lucía, Subtiava's parish church. The Spanish missionary Bartolomé de Las Casas preached here several times in the 16th century. Daisy explains that the people of Subtiava admired Las Casas because he defended the Indians, who were treated badly by the Spanish.

Everyone climbs aboard the horse-drawn cab, which is decorated today in honor of a convention taking place in León.

Above: The walking tours give Michael and his cousins plenty of places to explore. The church of Vera Cruz, with its ruins to climb among, is definitely one of this group's favorite spots.
Right: Spanish colonists built the church of Santa Lucía in 1530.

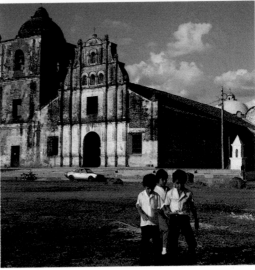

The immense tree known as El Tamarindo dwarfs the children playing at its base.

The next stop in the neighborhood of Subtiava is the giant tree called El Tamarindo. This tree is over 200 years old. It is famous because a rebel Indian chief was hanged from it by the Spanish. The people of Subtiava have always considered El Tamarindo one of their most important shrines — a symbol of their resistance against tyranny. Michael and his cousins know the story of El Tamarindo by heart.

The impressive Cathedral of León, built between 1746 and 1850, stands at the heart of the city.
Left inset: Lions on guard outside the church tempt the children to climb on them.
Right inset: Inside, huge oil paintings of the 14 stations of the cross cover the walls.

The Roman Catholic Cathedral of León is Michael's next stop. Daisy tells them that this is the largest church in Central America, and that it took 100 years to build. Near the cathedral's altar are two life-size lions sculpted in stone. These lions are symbols of the city, whose name, *León*, is Spanish for "lion." Michael sees the tomb of Rubén Darío, Nicaragua's national poet, at the foot of one of the lions. Darío died in 1916 but is honored even today. Outside of the cathedral, more sculpted lions stand guard. Michael and his cousins can't resist climbing on these, too.

Above: This former National Guard fortress served as a jail during the revolution.
Right: The statue of a street fighter throwing a grenade stands out front. Both monuments serve to remind the people of León of their struggle.

To finish their tour, Michael and his mother visit sites that remind them of the uprising of 1979. That year, the people of Nicaragua rose up in rebellion against the troops of the dictator Anastasio "Tachito" Somoza. In fierce hand-to-hand combat, the rebels in León defeated the government troops, but over a thousand people died in the battles. After León was free, the government air force retaliated by bombing the city. Several days later, the dictator fled the country, and a revolutionary army took power.

For Daisy and her family, the uprising of 1979 was a terrible sacrifice. Michael's father and over 40,000 other Nicaraguans died in the fighting. Today, Michael and his mother visit sites where the fiercest fighting took place in León. Even though Michael was born after his father died, the reminders of the revolution are everywhere around him.

A battered archway is all that remains of one of the many buildings destroyed in the 1979 revolution. It, too, is a stark reminder of the country's recent past.

Las Gigantonas: The Giant Puppets of León

Today, Michael and some of his friends are watching *Las Gigantonas* perform. The tradition of Las Gigantonas, or the giant puppets, is several hundred years old. The Nicaraguan Indians in León first created these puppets to make fun of their colonial masters, the Spanish. Often under the cover of darkness, Las Gigantonas have appeared in the streets, where they dance and entertain the people with music and comedy.

Over the years, the puppets have been used as a way to criticize the government. The street artists behind the puppets knew that humor was one way of keeping the people's spirits up in their struggle for liberty. The current puppet maker and keeper of Las Gigantonas is 71-year-old Doña Carmen Toruño de Garcia. Doña Carmen is training a new generation of Gigantona artists to continue the tradition.

Above: Doña Carmen keeps León's cherished tradition alive.
Below: A León crowd gathers around dancing Gigantona puppets. Crowd participation is as much a part of the tradition as the puppets are.

The colorful puppets surround their creator. In addition to being León's puppet maker, Doña Carmen is also famous for her knowledge of the area's history.

At the Market in León

Although Michael's grandfather grows some of the food that the Chávez family needs, the family still buys much of what it eats. This is especially true during the dry season, which lasts from November until May. For the food she must buy, Daisy shops at León's central fruit and vegetable market. Often, Michael goes along with her. At the market, the air bustles with activity, and he is fascinated by the hundreds of vendors who peddle their goods there.

Many vendors bring their fruits and vegetables to market in horse-drawn carts. Other vendors arrive by truck or automobile — even bus and taxi. Besides food, the vendors also offer goods such as home-made soap, clothes, flowers, and many other items. Michael stops to look at a pair of tennis shoes that catch his eye. He checks the price, hoping that maybe Daisy can buy him the shoes for his birthday.

The market overflows with enticing foods. Waiting patiently for his mother to select the fruits she wants, Michael hears his stomach growl.

Above: The market offers shoppers a dizzying variety of products. Left inset: A slow day for bread vendors. Right inset: Flowers splash the market with color.

Nicaraguans live on basic foods such as rice, red beans, onions, tomatoes, corn tortillas, plantains (a type of banana), and chicken or beef. The national dish of Nicaragua is called *gallo-pinto,* which is a spicy mixture of rice and red beans, usually fried with diced onions. Because of high food prices, most families can afford to eat meat only a few times a week.

33

Since León is located only 11 miles (18 km) from the Pacific Ocean, the market is always stocked with fresh fish. Michael's favorite seafood is fried conch fritters — a shellfish that is dipped in batter and fried. With its vast coastal areas, Nicaragua is hoping to develop shrimp and shellfish as bigger export items.

In the mornings, Nicaraguans often drink *café con leche,* which is coffee with heated milk. Coffee is the number one export crop in Nicaragua, but it's too hot around León to grow coffee. Instead, it's grown up north in the mountains.

A vendor, smiling from her neatly arranged market stall, uses a scale to measure out her customer's order. Displayed in front of her are several of Nicaragua's staple foods, including rice and red beans.

Sipping a cool refresco from a bolso, Michael is content to follow his mother through the market.

Another Nicaraguan tradition is the iced *refresco,* or fruit drink. Refrescos are commonly made from tamarind fruits, papayas, carrots, oranges, limes, guavas, mangoes, and pomegranates. On a hot day in León, there's nothing Michael likes better than a tall, icy *refresco natural* (natural fruit drink). On the streets, iced refrescos "to go" are poured into *bolsos,* or plastic bags.

The neighborhood marble champ follows his shot.   From the look on his opponent's face, Michael must be winning again.

Time Out for Sports

After doing his homework and chores, Michael still has time to play his favorite games and sports. He usually calls on his cousin Kelvin, who is also ten years old, because they like the same things: checkers, marbles, baseball, and soccer. Sometimes they play until they are exhausted and then collapse into the hammock, where they swing and talk until it is dark.

In the sports pages of the newspaper *Barricada*, Michael and Kelvin follow the progress of León's professional baseball team. This week, León's team is playing the team from Managua, the capital city, in a play-off game. The stadium in Managua, the largest in the country, holds 40,000 people. The boys also read about other games in Latin America's professional baseball leagues. The newspaper even reports on North American major-league baseball. Both Michael and Kelvin would like to see a major-league team play against a Nicaraguan all-star team.

The sports section of the daily newspaper *Barricada* is Michael's favorite section of the paper. Often, by the time he and Kelvin are finished poring over the day's baseball scores, there's not much left of the paper.

Today, Alicia beats both Michael and Kelvin to the newspaper. She's more interested in volleyball than in baseball and hopes to join a volleyball team as soon as she's old enough.

Michael's cousin, Alicia, who is five, says she wants to read the sports page, too. She has trouble reading some of the words, so Michael helps her. Alicia is interested in volleyball because some of the neighborhood women play on the city's volleyball team. After reading the sports page, they go out in the street to play ball. They use a stick for a bat because they don't have their own.

León has many sports teams. Basketball and volleyball are most popular with women and girls, but they also play soccer and baseball. For men and boys, León has formal leagues for baseball, soccer, basketball, volleyball, and boxing. The city also has junior leagues for the younger kids. On the weekends, every park and vacant lot in León has at least one game in progress.

Right: An enthusiastic volleyball player spikes the ball in a heated game on a León court. Below: Michael's baseball team — ready to hit the field — has a hard time holding still for the camera.

Even a crowded bus ride can't keep people from going to the beach today. The dog, however, decides to catch the next bus!

A Trip to the Pacific Ocean

Michael and Kelvin wake up excited today. They are going to the beach at Poneloya, which is 11 miles (18 km) by bus. Poneloya, which is a small fishing village on the Pacific Ocean, is also a popular weekend spot for tourists from León. Today, the bus is crowded, but Michael, Kelvin, Daisy, and Alicia don't mind. They are just glad to be getting away from León, where the temperature has risen to 100°F (37.8°C). In Poneloya, the ocean breezes will cool them.

They get off the bus at the south end of Poneloya, where an inland lagoon meets the ocean. Here, the water is calmer, and Michael, Kelvin, and Alicia can swim and play safely in the water. Just across the sand dunes, the waves of the Pacific Ocean are huge and treacherous.

Below: The beach, with its cool, wet sand, is the perfect place to play hopscotch.
Right: But the beach is best for splashing and swimming.

Michael and Kelvin meet several Poneloya boys who show them the fish they caught today. Because Michael has never been fishing, the young fishermen show him and Kelvin how to clean fish. The boys tell Michael that it's not as hard as it looks. It just takes practice. Sometimes Michael thinks it would be an adventure to live on the ocean. On the other hand, the boys from Poneloya say that they'd like to live in a big city such as León.

After another swim, everyone walks along the shore, picking up seashells of all shapes and sizes. Most of them are white, but some of them are shades of purple and orange. Michael and Kelvin stop to watch some of Poneloya's boat builders at work. There's so much to do at the beach that the boys wish the day were longer. The beach looks beautiful as the sun goes down, but today there's not enough time to watch. The last bus for León leaves at 5:00 p.m. As always, Michael and Kelvin drag their feet when Daisy calls.

◀ Because they live on the water, the Poneloya boys are skilled fishermen.
Inset: One of the young fishermen shows his new friends the quickest way to clean a fish.

Daisy and Michael poke cautiously at a shell beneath some rocks, looking for sand crabs.

Another group of boys, looking weary after a day of fishing, stops to talk with Michael.

After a relaxing day at the beach, Michael finds that the streets of downtown Léon seem noisy and crowded.

45

Sunday Afternoons at Michael's House

On Sunday afternoons, the entire Chávez and Garcia clan gathers to relax and visit. Under the shade of a laurel tree, Michael's grandfather Jésus is playing checkers with a neighborhood friend. Michael sits in the hammock, eating a warm, sweet tamale that he bought from a food vendor walking through San Jerónimo.

After working hard all week, Michael's aunts and uncles are glad to rest and talk over the week's activities. It is near the end of a long dry season, and everyone talks of the coming rain, hoping it will arrive soon. During the rainy season, which lasts from mid-May until November, it rains nearly every day. Then the temperatures drop, and everything turns a deep shade of green. Michael smiles, remembering the sound of rain on the roof.

Above: Michael's grandfather Jésus always makes time for a game of checkers.
Below: After a busy week, everyone enjoys a quiet Sunday afternoon. Even Michael and Kelvin seem willing to just sit awhile.

Michael wonders if his baby cousin Zuleyka will enjoy growing up in León as much as he does.

FOR YOUR INFORMATION: Nicaragua

Official Name: República de Nicaragua
(ray-POOH-blee-kah DAY nee-kuh-RAHG-wha)
Republic of Nicaragua

Capital: Managua (mah-NOG-wha)

History

The Early People of Nicaragua

Before the Spanish conquistadores came to Central and South America in the early 16th century, Nicaragua was one of the most populated areas in Central America. Many of the area's original people had migrated from North and South America. Others had come from the islands of the Caribbean. The Sumo, Miskito, and Rama Indians lived as food gatherers along Nicaragua's Atlantic coast. The Nicaraos, Chorotegas, and Lencas were farming tribes. They lived along the Pacific Ocean and the shores of the great lakes Colcibolcha and Xolotlán (now called Lake Nicaragua and Lake Managua).

León, as seen from above, is a sprawling mass of tiled roofs.

The Spanish Colonial Period

Spanish conquistadores Andrés Niño and Gil González Dávila reached the Nicaraguan lowlands from their base in Panama in 1522. Groups of peaceful Indians welcomed them and presented them with gold ornaments as gifts. The gold excited the Spaniards, who dreamed of getting rich. They decided to return to Panama, gather more soldiers, and conquer the whole area. The Spaniards returned several years later and established the first settlements in Nicaragua at Granada and León. Many of the native Indians resisted the Spanish invasion. But the conquistadores' superior weapons, as well as divisions among the Indian tribes, led the Spaniards to victory.

In 1573, the settlements at León and Granada came under the control of Spanish authorities in Guatemala. This ended the ties between the settlements and the Spaniards in Panama who had founded them. Of the two Nicaraguan settlements, Granada was the wealthier. Even so, León was chosen as the capital because its location on the Pacific Ocean gave it a better position for shipping and trade. Granada, on Lake Nicaragua, continued to grow because of its crops of sugarcane, cocoa, and indigo (a blue dye that was in great demand in Europe). Meanwhile, the people in León barely survived on their corn, bean, and rice crops.

The Spaniards were interested in Nicaragua partially because they were searching for a passageway to sail between the Atlantic and Pacific oceans. Some years earlier, the Spanish explorers had discovered that Lake Nicaragua was connected to the Atlantic Ocean by the San Juan River. Now, they sailed up and down Lake Nicaragua, hoping to find a similar passageway that would carry them through to the Pacific Ocean.

Throughout this period, most people in the country lived in the lowlands between the Pacific Ocean and the western shores of Lakes Nicaragua and Managua. The Spanish showed little interest in colonizing Nicaragua's Atlantic coast and northern forests. Instead, this area fell to the British and roving bands of pirates. In the 17th and 18th centuries, the British established colonies all along the coast. Through the colonies, they came to dominate the entire area.

Nicaragua Fights for Independence

In 1821, Central America claimed independence from Spain. Between 1823 and 1838, Nicaragua joined the republics of Guatemala, Honduras, El Salvador, and Costa Rica and formed the Central American Federation. The union remained weak because the republics quarreled over how the federation should be governed. After a series of conflicts, Nicaragua left the federation to form its own nation.

Inside Nicaragua, internal struggles raged between the *Criollos*, or native-born people of Nicaragua, and the Spanish-born landowners. Both groups wanted control of the country. This led to a rivalry between the country's two major cities, Granada and León, each of which served as headquarters for one of two developing political parties. León was the center for the Criollos, while Granada became headquarters for the Spanish landowners. Fierce battles took place between the supporters of the two parties.

The US Presence in Nicaragua in the 19th Century

In the midst of the confusion, California's gold rush of 1848 gave Nicaragua's economy an unexpected boost. At that time, Nicaragua became part of a "shortcut" between the eastern United States and California, bringing people and trade through the struggling country. As "gold fever" spread, thousands of fortune seekers made their way by wagon train to California. This overland route was long, difficult, and dangerous. The alternative, however, was to travel by ship around South America. The long voyage was often an even more hazardous journey.

The shortcut through Nicaragua was the brainstorm of US millionaire Cornelius Vanderbilt. In 1851, he established a steamship and stagecoach service called the Accessory Transit Company. Passengers traveled by boat from New York to Lake Nicaragua, took a stagecoach to Nicaragua's Pacific coast, and boarded a steamer bound for California. The Vanderbilt route cut through Nicaragua because the country offered the narrowest strip of land between the two oceans. This route quickly proved to be the fastest way to California's gold mines; within five years, over 100,000 people had traveled it.

The Rise and Fall of William Walker

In 1854, civil war erupted between the rival political groups based in Granada and León. The political group of León hired US soldier of fortune William Walker to lead their forces. Two years earlier, Walker, from Tennessee, had led an unsuccessful invasion of northern Mexico. There, seeking his fortune and claiming to be motivated by democratic ideals, Walker had tried to establish a new country. He now wanted to annex Nicaragua for the same reasons. The Criollos of León believed he was only interested in bringing democracy to the country.

In 1855, Walker and a band of 58 followers entered Nicaragua and easily captured Granada, thus ending the civil war. Abandoning his democratic beliefs, Walker set himself up as the country's new president. As he grew more powerful, he dreamed of conquering the other Central American countries, too. From these separate countries, Walker, now proslavery, planned to create one huge empire and annex it to the United States as new slave territory. Walker hoped that establishing new slave territory would strengthen the proslavery cause in the United States.

By this time, Walker had lost all support in Central America. The other Central American countries banded together to defeat him. When Walker's forces next invaded Costa Rica, a combined Costa Rican and Central American volunteer army was waiting for them. Walker's army met defeat at the Battle of Rivas. To avoid being killed by the enraged Central Americans, Walker surrendered to the US Navy. He later made two further attempts to reconquer Nicaragua and parts of Honduras. He was finally captured and later executed by Honduran authorities on September 12, 1860.

US Interventions, 1909-1934

In 1893, José Santós Zelaya came to power in Nicaragua. Many of his policies changed Nicaragua's economy, political system, and way of life. He increased coffee production, established a written constitution, set up tax reforms, introduced public education, and built a system of roads, ports, telegraph lines, and railroads. Although Zelaya's actions brought economic growth to the country, many people saw him as a tyrant. His government was corrupt, and many of his ventures served only to bring him or his officials wealth. Zelaya took away many of the Indians' communal lands, and anyone who opposed him was harassed, jailed, or even killed.

In addition to being oppressive within Nicaragua, however, Zelaya backed revolutions in other Central American countries. He also angered the United States when he held discussions with France, Britain, and Japan about building a transoceanic canal across Nicaragua. This was Zelaya's retaliation against the United States for its decision to build a canal through Panama instead of Nicaragua. For all these reasons, when two US citizens were killed in Nicaragua in 1909, the United States seized the opportunity to send marines into the country. Zelaya resigned and fled Nicaragua.

For the next 24 years, the United States supervised the Nicaraguan government. Resistance to the US presence led to another rebellion in 1911, and the US Marines again entered the country and remained until 1933. Between 1927 and 1933, Nicaraguan rebels, led by General Augusto César Sandino, kept up their resistance to the US presence. To deal with the rebels, the United States established and trained the Nicaraguan National Guard. As the US Marines prepared to leave the country in 1933, Anastasio Somoza became head of the National Guard. From this position, Somoza took control of the country. A year later, members of his National Guard murdered Sandino as he was leaving government peace talks. Sandino became the martyr of modern Nicaraguan history.

Nicaragua's Current History

Somoza had himself named president in 1936, beginning a family dictatorship that ruled Nicaragua in a brutal fashion for almost 50 years. Anyone who tried to change the system was tortured or killed. Between 1960 and 1970, living conditions became unbearable for the majority of the people. A new opposition group called the Sandinista Front for National Liberation (FSLN) emerged. This group, named after General Sandino and known as Sandinistas, included church and middle-class people as well as farmers, students, and the poor. In a mass uprising in 1979, the Sandinistas overthrew the Somoza dictatorship. After five years of heavy fighting, the people were jubilant. But the human toll of the war was staggering: 40,000 people had died; 100,000 were wounded.

Nicaragua's ruling class, and eventually the US government, opposed the Sandinista revolution, claiming that the Sandinistas were also dictators who intended to lead revolution in the neighboring countries of Guatemala, El Salvador, and Honduras. A large, counter-revolutionary ("contra") army emerged, intent on overthrowing the government or forcing it to change its policies. In the early 1980s, the United States spent millions of dollars funding, equipping, and training the contras. Later, when US government officials became divided over this funding, money for military spending was banned and only humanitarian funding was continued. Many members of the Nicaraguan middle class, alarmed since their standard of living has fallen, also sided with the contras. The Sandinistas, however, insisted that the contra war caused the country's economic problems.

In 1984, national elections were held in Nicaragua. Voters gave the Sandinistas 68% of the votes, electing Daniel Ortega Saavedra as Nicaragua's president. Between 1981 and 1990, the contras waged a continuous war against the Nicaraguan government. Based in Honduras, the contras kidnapped and killed thousands of Nicaraguans. The war also cost billions of dollars in economic losses. Peace talks that began in 1987 reduced the fighting, but Nicaragua remains a country of political turmoil. In 1989, other countries of the region, including Honduras, joined Nicaragua in calling for the dismantling of the contras in an effort to reduce the strife in Nicaragua and in neighboring countries.

In February of 1990, nearly two dozen political parties joined the Sandinistas on the ballot for the national and local elections. Like the 1984 elections, these were closely supervised by foreign election monitors. In the presidential election, Daniel Ortega was defeated by Violeta Barrios de Chamorro, leader of the National Opposition Union (UNO), a group of 14 political parties opposed to the Sandinistas. Chamorro had once been sympathetic to the Sandinista revolution and was even a member of the group that took over power from the Somoza dictatorship. But soon after the takeover in 1979, she split from the

Sandinistas and became a member of the opposition. Many Nicaraguans voted against the Sandinistas because of the nation's troubled economy. But many also believed that US policies against the Sandinistas, including funding the contra war, contributed to Nicaragua's economic hardships.

Government

From the overthrow of Somoza in 1979 until 1984, Nicaragua was governed by a committee of leaders who had participated in the armed struggle against Somoza. Since 1984, Nicaragua has had a constitution that has called for a democratically elected government. Everyone 16 years old and over has the right to vote. The government consists of three branches: executive, legislative, and judicial. The head of the executive branch of the government is the president, who is elected for a six-year term. The president and majority party select government ministers and other high appointed officials.

The highest legislative body in the country is the National Assembly, which has 96 members. The members are elected for six-year terms by proportional vote. Proportional voting means that if a political party gets 10% of the votes, it receives 10% of the seats.

The judicial system of Nicaragua is headed by a supreme court. Its seven members are selected by the National Assembly for six-year terms. Below the supreme court, the system also includes regional and local courts.

In 1987, the National Assembly established a new constitution after discussions held throughout the country. Nicaragua's constitution defines the government's structure and guarantees the citizens certain economic, social, and political rights, although the National Assembly suspended some of these rights by emergency degree during the contra war.

Climate

Nicaragua is a hot, tropical country. The wet, warm winds of the Atlantic Ocean drop large amounts of rain on the Atlantic coastal lowlands. The southern zone of this coast receives up to 240 inches (610 cm) of rain annually. With all this rain, the dry season on the Atlantic coast is short, but the rest of the country is quite dry from November to May.

On the Pacific side of the country, farmers plant and harvest crops during the rainy season, which lasts from mid-May until November. In the mountainous higher elevations, the temperature is somewhat cooler. There it is possible to grow coffee, the country's major export.

NICARAGUA — Political and Physical

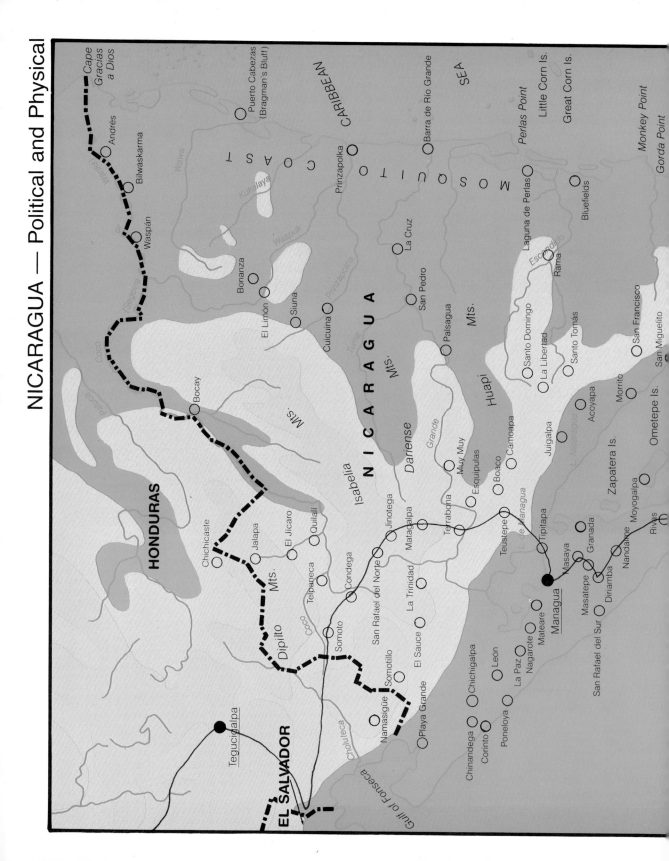

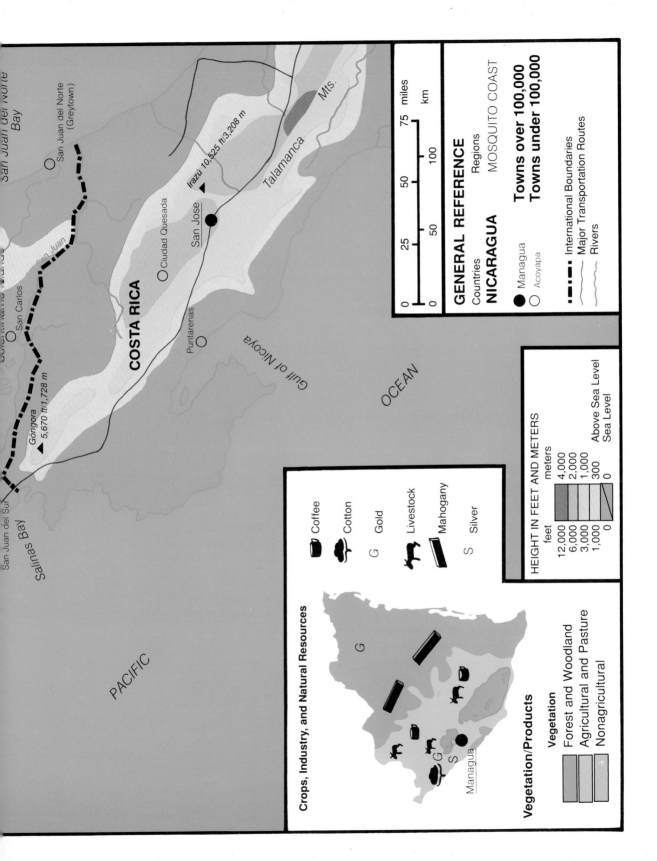

PACIFIC OCEAN

Gulf of Nicoya

Salinas Bay

San Juan del Sur

Góngora ▲ 5,670 ft/1,728 m

San Juan del Norte Bay

San Juan del Norte (Greytown)

San Carlos

San Juan

COSTA RICA

Ciudad Quesada

San José

Puntarenas

Irazú 10,525 ft/3,208 m ▲

Talamanca Mts.

GENERAL REFERENCE

Countries   Regions
NICARAGUA   MOSQUITO COAST

● Managua   **Towns over 100,000**
○ Acoyapa   **Towns under 100,000**

▬ ∙ ▬ ∙ ▬ International Boundaries
———   Major Transportation Routes
～～～   Rivers

miles				
0	25	50	75	miles
0	50	100		km

HEIGHT IN FEET AND METERS

feet   meters
12,000   4,000
6,000   2,000
3,000   1,000
1,000   300   Above Sea Level
0   0   Sea Level

Crops, Industry, and Natural Resources

● Coffee
● Cotton
G Gold
🐂 Livestock
▱ Mahogany
S Silver

Managua

Vegetation/Products

Vegetation
▮ Forest and Woodland
▮ Agricultural and Pasture
▮ Nonagricultural

Land

Nicaragua, the largest country in Central America, covers about 57,000 square miles (148,000 sq km) of land. It is approximately the same size as the US state of Georgia and somewhat larger than the Canadian provinces of Nova Scotia and New Brunswick combined. Nicaragua has 336 miles (541 km) of coastline on the Atlantic Ocean and 219 miles (352 km) on the Pacific Ocean. Honduras lies to the north; Costa Rica lies to the south. Only about one-third of the country's farmland is being put to use. The country's small population and its lack of money for agricultural development have kept the land uncultivated.

Three basic geographical regions make up the country: a triangular-shaped mountainous area that extends from the Honduras border to the border of Costa Rica; a coastal lowland on the Atlantic side of the country; and another lowland on the Pacific side. Near the Pacific side are Nicaragua's Lake Managua and Lake Nicaragua. These are the two largest lakes in Central America. Lake Managua is 32 miles (52 km) long and 15 miles (25 km) wide at its widest. Lake Nicaragua is 92 miles (148 km) long and 34 miles (55 km) wide. A string of 40 volcanoes stretches across the country's Pacific coast.

Natural Resources, Agriculture, and Industry

Nicaragua's major natural resources include its fertile soil, its tropical climate, its extensive forests, and the oceans off its coasts. Sea life is abundant off both the Atlantic and Pacific coasts. Energy comes from the heat of volcanic thermal springs (geothermal power) as well as the waters of some of its rivers, which are harnessed to produce electricity (hydroelectric power). Nicaragua has large deposits of copper, silver, lead, zinc, and gold, which has become a major export. Engineers have found no major gas or petroleum deposits, but they continue to explore this possibility. Nicaragua's location — another natural resource — makes it ideal for a transoceanic canal. Government and business leaders are currently discussing plans to build one. This could mean thousands of jobs for Nicaragua and a boost to the economy.

Unlike other nations in mountainous Central America, Nicaragua can devote 70% of its land to farming and grazing. Agricultural industries account for over 45% of the Nicaraguan work force. The country's major agricultural products are coffee, cotton, cattle and other livestock, sugarcane, corn, beans, rice, bananas, garlic, citrus fruits, and sorghum. In the past, fish, crayfish, shrimp, and other shellfish were available only for consumption, but recently these foods have also become major export items. Since 1979, the government has determined what kinds of farms will exist in Nicaragua. It set up state farms on the land taken from Somoza and other wealthy landowners and set aside other wealthy landowners and set aside other land for cooperatives made up of groups of farmers. It also set aside land for peasant farmers.

Because of its forests and mines, Nicaragua has thriving mining, timber, and construction industries. It also has chemical, textile, cement, petroleum-refining, and food-processing industries. In the years following the 1979 revolution, the government controlled mining as well as other major sectors of the economy, such as banks, public transportation, foreign trade, and telecommunications. Moreover, it decided which products to export. In total, the government controlled about 40% of the economy, deciding what wages people received, what prices could be charged for rent and for products, and who would receive loans and other financial help. The government also instituted a progressive income tax, which means that the more one makes, the more taxes one pays.

Years of war have damaged Nicaragua's economy. Under its wartime budget, defense spending rose from only 7% of the national budget to over 45%. This left little money for education, health services, and other investments that might help build the country's economy. A too-rigid following of Marxist economics also hurt the country, according to some critics of then President Ortega's policies. At a time when communist nations such as the Soviet Union were becoming more economically flexible, Nicaragua apparently was not. As a consequence of governmental decisions and the war, Nicaragua is at this time the poorest nation in the Western Hemisphere.

Education

Until the 1979 revolution, Nicaragua's schools received little money from the government. Before then, over 50% of all Nicaraguans could neither read nor write. The Sandinista government, however, launched a massive literacy campaign. While this campaign was intended, in part, to promote the causes of the Sandinista revolution, it also, with the help of thousands of volunteer teachers, reduced Nicaragua's illiteracy rate to 12%. This campaign has made the people of Nicaragua some of the best-educated people in Central America.

Education and health care have become the government's most important priorities. To improve the educational system, the government has built more schools, hired more teachers, and eliminated school tuition. School uniforms, books, and most other supplies are provided by the government. Because of these changes, student enrollment has doubled since 1979. Also since the revolution, a free school lunch program, kindergartens, and day-care centers for the children of working mothers are being developed. Of course, all services such as these must be paid for through taxes paid by the governed, which is not a small expense for an economy already weakened by a costly civil war.

Religion

Most Nicaraguans are Roman Catholics, but 85 different Protestant faiths are practiced in the country as well. Along the Atlantic coast, which was under British influence for years, many people attend Protestant churches. Many of Nicaragua's churches and church members were active in the struggle to overthrow the Somoza dictatorship, and several high-ranking Sandinista government officials were Catholic priests. While many priests and nuns supported the revolution, the church leaders sometimes clashed with Sandinista leaders over many of the government's social and economic policies.

Population and Ethnic Groups

With about 65 people per square mile (25 people per sq km), Nicaragua is the least densely populated country in Central America. It has a population of 3.3 million, 86% of whom are *mestizos* — people of mixed Spanish-Indian heritage. Another 8% are blacks, 4% are Indians, and a small percentage are direct descendants of Europeans. The blacks and Indians live primarily along the coast of the Atlantic. Many of the blacks are descendants of Africans who were brought to the Caribbean islands and Central America as slaves.

Language

Spanish is Nicaragua's official language, but many people along the Atlantic coast speak English, as well as dialects of Spanish, Creole, and Indian. Schools in this area teach classes in English or native dialects and offer Spanish as a second language. This is unusual in Central America, where nearly everyone speaks Spanish. English dominates the Atlantic coast because the British controlled the area from 1625 to 1885. The mountains and dense forests have kept the people of the Pacific and Atlantic coasts separate until recently. Because the people have not mixed, their languages have not mixed either.

Art and Culture

Nicaragua is a nation that values art, music, and literature. Their love of literature is clear even to the tourist because of the way the people honor some of the country's famous novelists and poets. One of the most famous and popular Latin American poets was the Nicaraguan poet Rubén Darío (1867-1916), born in San Pedro de Metapa. Through his work, Darío brought a sense of pride to the poetry of Latin America that gave Hispanic poetry a character of its own. His style inspired many poets who continue to write and often read aloud in public gatherings. In his honor, the people of Nicaragua renamed his birthplace Ciudad Darío and established the country's highest poetry award in his name. The Rubén Darío National Theater in Managua, which hosts musical, theatrical, and dance performances, also honors the poet.

Music in Nicaragua grows from both the past and the present. Folk and contemporary styles of music are especially popular in the cities and towns. More traditional forms have survived as well, especially in the rural areas. There, the music has a more traditional sound because the people use pre-Columbian instruments such as the *maraca*, a rattlelike instrument made from a gourd; the *chirimia*, a clarinet; and even instruments made from animal horns.

Sports and Recreation

Nicaraguans have made baseball their country's national sport. Their enthusiasm for the game is apparent by the fact that most newspapers follow the North American major-league teams as well as the Nicaraguan teams. But Nicaraguans are not just spectators; they are also eager to play, and teams form at all levels, from local junior leagues to national leagues. Soccer is also popular, as are volleyball, boxing, basketball, track and field, and table tennis. Women are as active as men in many of these sports, and in the evenings, it is common to see sporting events of one type or another taking place in nearly every park or vacant lot.

Currency

The national currency of Nicaragua is the córdoba. The córdoba was named in 1912 in honor of the explorer Francisco Fernández de Córdoba. There are 100 *centavos* to the córdoba, but centavo coins are rarely used today.

A 5,000-córdoba note.

Managua

The capital city of Nicaragua is Managua, which has an official population of over one million people. The government moved the capital from León to Managua in 1858. As the capital, Managua is the seat of the government as well as the nation's center of commerce and industry.

In 1972, a terrible earthquake nearly destroyed the city. It suffered further destruction during the revolution of 1979 when President Somoza was overthrown. Because of the wartime lack of resources, much of the capital remains in ruins. Also because of the war, the city's population has grown rapidly in the 1980s, with war refugees moving into urban neighborhoods. Located on Lake Managua, the city is now home to over one-third of the nation's population.

Nicaraguans in North America

Approximately 250,000 Nicaraguan refugees now live in the United States. Many of these people left their country because they disagreed with the Sandinista revolution. Others sought the economic advantages that the United States can offer. The majority of Nicaraguans in the United States live in Florida. In fact, the city of Miami has more Nicaraguans than any other city besides Managua. Many of these refugees have families still living in Nicaragua.

The majority of Nicaraguans now living in Canada have moved there since 1986. Many of these people, like many of those in the United States, also left their homeland because of its economic situation. In Canada, the Nicaraguans hope that they will find opportunities that Nicaragua cannot presently offer. Canada's Nicaraguan population tends to remain in the larger cities, with Toronto, Montreal, and Ottawa having the largest concentrations.

More Books about Nicaragua

Enchantment of Central America: Nicaragua. Carpenter and Balow (Childrens Press)
Fodor's Central America. (Fodor's Travel Publications)
Nicaragua. Hanmer. (Franklin Watts)
Nicaragua in Pictures. (Lerner Publications)
Nicaragua: Struggling with Change. Adams (Dillon Press)

Glossary of Useful Nicaraguan (Spanish) Words

beisbol (BAYZ-bohl)............................baseball
bolsos (BOLE-sohs).............................plastic bags
cajeta (kah-HAY-tuh)..........................candy
chi-cha (CHEE-chah)..........................sweetened corn drink
escuela (es-QWAY-lah).......................school
este (ES-teh) ....east
futbol (FUTE-bohl) ....soccer
gallo-pinto (GUY-yoh PIHN-toh)............"painted rooster," name of staple dish consisting of rice, beans, and spices
Gigantonas (he-gann-TONE-ahs).........giant puppets

juego (HWAY-goh)	....	game
mango (MAHN-goh)	....	a delicious tropical fruit
mar (mahr)	....	sea
norte (NOHR-teh)	....	north
oeste (oh-ES-teh)	....	west
plátano (PLAH-tah-noh)	....	banana
Semana Santa		
(seh-MAHN-ah sahn-tah)	....	Holy Week — the week before Easter
sur (suhr)	....	south
tamale (tah-MAHL-ee)	....	seasoned ground meat rolled in cornmeal dough or corn husks and steamed

Things to Do — Research Projects

Nicaragua is a country that has rich and varied cultural traditions mixing the influences of its Native American and Spanish heritage. It is also a country that has seen more than its share of political turmoil and strife. Especially since it won its independence from Spain in the 1800s, Nicaragua has attracted the attention of the other nations of the Americas. It has been viewed as a "shortcut" between the Atlantic and Pacific oceans, and as a place where outside political forces might extend their influence. Today, both the United States and other countries have made their desires known in Nicaragua. The United States, in particular, has attempted in recent years to influence the political outlook in Nicaragua through its on-again, off-again support of the contras.

To best understand Nicaragua, then, it is important to have up-to-date information. For that reason, current newspapers and magazines could be useful sources of information. Two publications your library may have will tell you about recent magazine and newspaper articles on many topics:

Readers' Guide to Periodical Literature
Children's Magazine Guide

For accurate answers to questions about such topics of current interest as Nicaragua's political situation, look up *Nicaragua* in one of these publications. They will lead you to up-to-date information.

1. Nicaragua's location between the Atlantic and Pacific oceans has played a role in the country's development. The United States once considered building a canal through Nicaragua instead of through Panama. Why is Nicaragua's location so important? Where would you have built a canal?

2. The Sandinistas and the contras are the two main groups that have recently struggled for control of Nicaragua. Find out more about each group, its ideas, and its goals.

3. Research US involvement in Nicaragua both past and present. Take a stand on the issue of current US involvement — pro or con — and defend it.

4. Historically Nicaragua is home to several Indian tribes such as the Miskitos, the Ramas, and the Sumos. Pick a tribe that interests you and learn all you can about it.

More Things to Do — Activities

1. Michael lives in an extended family. He and his mother share a house with his grandparents, aunts, uncles, and cousins. In some places, it is more common for people to live in a nuclear family. In this type of family, only a father, mother, and their children live together. Talk with someone whose family life is different from your own.

2. Learn more about Nicaraguan foods. Which of their foods are unfamiliar to you? Which of your foods might seem strange to them? You might want to plan a "typical" Nicaraguan meal.

3. Compare Michael's life to your own. Discuss the ways in which they are alike or different.

4. If you would like a pen pal in Nicaragua, write to:

International Pen Friends
P.O. Box 290065
Brooklyn, NY 11229

Worldwide Pen Friends
P.O. Box 39097
Downey, CA 90241

Be sure to tell them what country you want your pen pal to be from. Also include your full name, age, and address.

Michael, the boy from León, says goodbye.

Index